Tough Guys

Tough Guys

Eric Zweig

James Lorimer & Company, Ltd., Publishers
Toronto

James Lorimer & Company Ltd. acknowledges the support of the Canada Council for the Arts and the Ontario Arts Council for our publishing program.
We acknowledge the financial support of the Government of Canada through the Book Publishing Industry Development Program (BPIDP) for our publishing activities. We acknowledge the Government of Ontario through the Ontario Media Development Corporation's Ontario Book Initiative.

Cover design by: Meredith Bangay

Library and Archives Canada Cataloguing in Publication

Zweig, Eric, 1963-
    Tough guys : hockey rivals in times of war and disaster / Eric Zweig

(Recordbooks)
Includes bibliographical references.
ISBN 978-1-55277-428-1 (bound).--ISBN 978-1-55277-423-6 (pbk.)

    1. Stanley Cup (Hockey)--History--Juvenile literature. 2. Influenza Epidemic, 1918-1919--Juvenile literature. I. Title. II. Series: Record books

GV847.7.Z84 2009   j796.962'648   C2009-901662-1

James Lorimer & Company Ltd.,
Publishers
317 Adelaide Street West, Suite #1002
Toronto, ON
M5V 1P9
www.lorimer.ca

Distributed in the United States by:
Orca Book Publishers
P.O. Box 468
Custer, WA USA
98240-0468

Printed and bound in Canada.

Contents

In Memory of BB, our tough little guy.

Prologue

The most famous name in hockey history is not the name of a player. It's not the name of a team. It's the name of a trophy — the Stanley Cup.

The Stanley Cup is named after Lord Stanley of Preston. Lord Stanley was the Governor General of Canada from 1888 to 1893. He had played many sports growing up in England, and found new ones to enjoy in Canada. Lord Stanley saw his first hockey game in 1889. Soon, some of his children started playing. His daughter Isobel became one of the first female hockey players in Canada.

Lord Stanley donated the Stanley Cup in 1893. Hockey already had lots of fans, but the new trophy made the sport even more popular. Soon, there were hockey leagues all across Canada. There were some in the United States too.

The Stanley Cup was much smaller back then. It was only the size of the bowl that's on top of the trophy today. It had a black base with a silver band. The silver band was where the name of the winning team was engraved. Soon, the names of the winning players got engraved too. Adding new silver bands to fit all the names is how the Stanley Cup got so big.

Today, the Stanley Cup stands nearly three feet tall (89.5 cm). It weighs nearly 35 pounds (15.5 kg). It's pretty heavy … but not so heavy that players can't pick it up! The winners always lift it over their heads and skate around the ice. Other traditions help make the Stanley Cup special. Everyone on the winning team gets his own day to take the Cup home. The Cup always draws a big crowd when

Sir Frederick Arthur Stanley, Lord Stanley of Preston, left the Cup as a gift to Canada in 1893.

the players show it off.

At first, no one league controlled the Stanley Cup. There were many smaller leagues in Canada, and their champions could challenge for the Stanley Cup. Stanley Cup games always got lots of attention. Arenas in the old days held a few thousand. Today, NHL arenas hold nearly 20,000 fans. There was no TV or Internet back then. There wasn't even radio. But newspapers were filled with stories. People would gather together to get updates by telegraph. Often, they had to wait in the cold outside a newspaper or telegraph office just to hear the score. But people did it. They loved their hockey!

A lot has changed over the years. Whole leagues have come and gone. Two world wars have been fought. Yet the Stanley Cup is still here. In all the years since 1893 there have been only two times when the Stanley Cup wasn't presented. The most recent time was in 2004–05. There was a bitter battle about money between players and team owners. A lockout wiped out the entire hockey season. It angered fans everywhere.

The reasons the Stanley Cup was cancelled in 1919 were very different. The 1918–19 hockey season had started with cheerful celebrations. After nearly five long years, World War I had finally ended. But the war had nearly killed pro hockey.

The Cup Goes Pro

Only amateur teams played for the Stanley Cup until 1906. By 1914, hockey's two top professional leagues met in the Stanley Cup Final. There was the National Hockey Association (NHA) in the east. The Pacific Coast Hockey Association (PCHA) was out west. The National Hockey League replaced the NHA in 1917. By 1927, the NHL was the only league playing for the Stanley Cup.

Many players quit the game to become soldiers. Many fans stopped going to the rink.

And just as World War I was ending, an awful disease spread across the globe. It was known as the Spanish Influenza, or Spanish Flu. About 50,000 Canadians died of the Spanish Flu. About 50 million people died all around the world. In 1919, the Spanish Flu turned the struggle for the Stanley Cup into a true battle of life and death.

1 Bad Joe from Brandon

Right from the start, hockey was fast and exciting. The game always had star players. Joe Hall's hockey career began not long after the Stanley Cup started. He was still going strong in 1919. That made him one of the oldest players in hockey. He was also one of the roughest!

Trouble seemed to follow Joe Hall. Bad Joe, they called him. Or sometimes just Bad Man. His friends said he wasn't as bad as all that. As he got older, he tried to stay within the rules. It was never easy for him. Other players always tried to get him riled up. "He wants to play clean hockey," the *Winnipeg Tribune* reported. "But how can he when other players try to slash and cut him?"

Was Joe Hall a dirty player, or just a tough one? "I don't think I'm as bad as I'm painted," Joe once said. "But I can take care of myself if anybody starts anything!"

Joe Hall was born in England on May 3, 1882, but he grew up in Winnipeg. In 1900, Joe joined a hockey team in Brandon, Manitoba, but hockey seemed to take him somewhere new every winter.

In November 1905, Joe signed his first pro contract with Portage Lake. The team from Michigan was part of the International Hockey League (IHL). The IHL was known for its rough brand of hockey. Joe fit in perfectly! He led Portage Lake to the league championship of the

1905–06 season. He also led the league with 98 penalty minutes.

Joe's reputation as hockey's Bad Man grew when he returned to Manitoba. Joe made headlines all across Canada for his rough play in a game on December 18, 1907. "Hall deliberately struck [Bert] Boulton in the face with his stick and broke his nose," reported the *Toronto Star*. "Upon returning to the ice, Hall struck [Charlie] Tobin on the head. He cut his

Tick, Tack, Toe

Joe Hall had a neighbour in Brandon named George Tackaberry. George was a shoemaker. Around 1905, Joe helped George design better-fitting hockey skates. Their new skates became very popular. In 1937, the CCM sporting goods company bought the design. "Tacks" remained the best name in hockey skates for many, many years.

A Joe Hall hockey card from the 1910–1911 National Hockey Association (NHA) season.

scalp open four inches and knocked him senseless."

Even in a rough sport like hockey, Joe's actions could not be ignored. He was kicked out of the pro league in Manitoba.

For the next few seasons, Joe bounced

from team to team and league to league. His temper continued to get him in trouble. Soon his skills started to suffer. When Joe joined the Quebec Bulldogs in 1910–11, he played in only 10 of the team's 16 games. He didn't score a single goal.

Joe Who?

The Quebec Bulldogs had two stars named Joe. Joe Hall anchored the defence. Joe Malone was their top scorer. People called Malone "Phantom Joe" for his tricky moves. He seemed to disappear and reappear like a ghost. In his best season with the Bulldogs, Malone scored 43 goals in just 20 games! Later, with the Montreal Canadiens, Malone scored 44 goals in 20 games the 1917–18 NHL season. Malone's 44 goals were an NHL record for many years. Maurice Richard finally broke the record. He scored 50 goals for the Canadiens in 1944–45. But it took him a full 50-game season to do it.

The Bulldogs played in the National Hockey Association (NHA), the top league in hockey. The Bulldogs decided to give Joe one last chance. He repaid them with a brilliant season. According to a Quebec City newspaper, playing on a winning team turned him into one of the best defenceman in the game. He had found a new hockey home.

2 Rivals in a Rough Game

Joe Hall played all 18 games on the Quebec Bulldogs schedule in 1911–12, scoring 15 goals. The Bulldogs won the Stanley Cup that season. They won it again the next year too. In 1914, Quebec fans voted Joe the team's most popular player. Sometimes, though, Joe's temper still got the better of him … especially when he played against Newsy Lalonde.

Newsy Lalonde's real first name was Edouard. He got his nickname when he

Newsy Lalonde's hockey card from the 1910–1911 NHA season.

had to go to work in a newsprint factory as a boy. Lalonde grew up to become the greatest hockey player of his time. Everywhere he went he scored a lot of goals. He also piled up a lot of penalty minutes. His fans would pack the home arena to cheer him on. Fans in other cities screamed, "Get Lalonde!" when he came to town.

"If you think hockey is a tough game now," Newsy would say when he was older, "you have no idea what toughness is!"

Like Joe Hall, Newsy seemed to play for a new team in a new league almost every winter. He finally found a home when he joined the brand new Montreal Canadiens in 1909. He starred with the Canadiens for nearly 13 years.

Montreal had been the top city in hockey since 1875. Yet in all that time, nearly every team in Montreal had been an English team. The Canadiens were not the first French team in Montreal, but they quickly became the best. Today, the Canadiens are the only team from the first NHA season that still exists in the NHL. They have won the Stanley Cup more often than any other team in hockey history. Sometimes sportswriters still call the team the Flying Frenchmen. That

A Star is Born

Newsy Lalonde grew up in Ontario, but his family was French Canadian. He was born in Cornwall on October 31, 1887. His family was poor. Newsy didn't get his first pair of skates until he was 13 years old. "We didn't have a rink in our neighbourhood," Newsy recalled. "So we played wherever there was ice. The street, a pond, whatever. After a while, I really started to get good." He was good enough to sign his first pro contract when he was only 18.

nickname dates all the way back to the time of speedy stars like Newsy Lalonde and his teammates.

Newsy could play anywhere on the ice, but he usually lined up at centre. He was always one of the top scorers in the NHA. Joe Hall was always one of the league's top defencemen. It was only natural they'd have their battles. Newsy and Joe became bitter enemies on the ice.

Newsy blamed Joe for most of their fights. "Hall always starts chewing the rag the minute he sees my face," he explained. "I never speak to him until he shouts at me half a dozen times. He keeps telling me I won't finish the game. Then, of course, I've got to start something."

But Joe's story to the press was the opposite. "I never had anything against Newsy," he claimed. "He began the whole thing one game. He kept up a running fire of insults. I became sore and now I always hand him back the same lines. I body him hard on every occasion and goad him on to hitting me. Then I strike back."

Who was telling the truth? Who knows? But nobody was surprised that the two went at it when Newsy's Canadiens faced Joe's Bulldogs on the night of December 30, 1913. The Canadiens beat the Bulldogs 4–3. "The game was rather slow," reported the *Montreal Star*. "But it was rough."

Late in the first period, Newsy whacked Joe in the head with his stick. Nobody wore helmets in those days. Newsy's high stick cut Joe for eight stitches. "It was a disgraceful scene," said the *Star*. Newsy said Joe had been jamming his stick into his ribs since the opening faceoff. But Newsy was the one who got kicked out of the game. Both players were fined $15. (That would be worth about $300 today!)

The two teams met again in Montreal on January 14. George Kennedy was the owner of the Canadiens. He asked the president of the NHA to speak to both players before the game. "With a good warning to each of them, I'm sure you'll prevent possible bloodshed and bodily harm."

There was no rough stuff at all in the first period. It ended with the Canadiens ahead 2–0. Early in the second, Joe chased after Newsy. Joe tripped Newsy and got a minor penalty. Later in the period, the puck bounced behind the net. Newsy

"Bad Man" and "Newsy" Enemies For Years Will Get Warning This Time

JOE HALL and "Newsy" Lalonde, whose hockey meetings for years have been marked by fights. The Canadien management fears bloodshed when they meet this week, and has asked President Quinn to personally warn each of the pair.

"NEWSY" LALONDE   JOE HALL

This story appeared in the Montreal Herald *the day before the Canadiens–Bulldogs game on January 14, 1914.*

chased after it. Joe chased after him. What happened next is not really clear, but the results were painful. Newsy crashed hard into the boards. His head was cut in two places. His teammates had to help him off the ice. Newsy wouldn't return that night. He needed ten stitches to close his wounds.

Newsy was sure Joe had hurt him on purpose. "I heard he was offering to bet $500 I wouldn't finish the game." The referees blamed Joe too. They kicked him out for the rest the game, and fined him again for $15. Most newspapers claimed that Joe hit Newsy from behind with his stick. Yet, even in Montreal, some fans thought it was a clean hit. Others said it wasn't even Joe that hit Newsy.

"I swear I did not hit Lalonde with my stick," Joe told reporters after the game. "I would not have done so for $500. Especially not after what Kennedy said."

"I love this game of hockey," Hall went on, "… Here I am with my head cut, my two wrists bandaged, and both my legs hurt. Yet I play because I love the game and because my teammates need me. If I ever played a fair, square game, I played it tonight. I never lifted my stick to Lalonde. If I am responsible for his injuries, it was through a clean body check."

There were lots of stories in the Montreal papers saying that Joe should be suspended. The president of the NHA didn't agree. "If it had been any other two players," he said, "the incident would have been passed off as an ordinary piece of rough play."

Still, it was hard to imagine that Joe and Newsy could ever be friends. Or even teammates. Yet strange things would soon happen to hockey. The world was about to go to war. World War I changed a lot about life in Canada. Hockey was no exception.

3 Good for Morale

The "war" between Joe Hall and Newsy Lalonde was soon to be replaced by the real thing. The 1913–14 hockey season was the last one before World War I began. The Toronto Blueshirts of the NHA won the Stanley Cup that year. Scotty Davidson was their captain. He seemed to have a bright future in front of him. But when training camp opened in the fall of 1914, Scotty was no longer with the Blueshirts. He was with the army.

World War I began in August 1914. Germany attacked Belgium, and then England and France declared war on Germany. Soon, many more countries were drawn into the fighting. Canada was part of the British Empire. So when England was at war, Canada was too. Few people knew how long and horrible the war would be. Many thought it would be over by Christmas. They did not want to miss their chance to fight. By September, more than 32,000 Canadians had joined the army.

The war did not end that Christmas. It dragged on for many more years. In time, more than 600,000 Canadians fought. Fit, strong men were always needed. Young hockey players were expected to sign up. Scotty Davidson was only the first. By 1916, all the best amateur hockey leagues had teams with hockey-playing soldiers. Hockey was a good way for soldiers to stay fit for army service. Eventually, even the NHA had a team of soldiers.

A lot of sports leagues shut down in Canada. There were just too many athletes (and too many sports fans) fighting overseas. Some people felt the pro hockey leagues should shut down too. Others believed that hockey was good for morale. Following their favourite hockey teams was an easy way for people to forget their troubles, if only for a while. Stars like Joe Hall and Newsy Lalonde kept things interesting for NHA fans. Frank Foyston helped keep up the excitement for fans of the Pacific Coast Hockey Association (PCHA).

Frank had once been a teammate of Scotty Davidson. He scored a key goal in the final game when the Blueshirts won the Stanley Cup in 1914. "Foyston was the best man on the ice," the *Toronto Star* said. "He's been going great guns lately, but he

Frank Foyston in the green, red and white-striped uniform of the Seattle Metropolitans.

never played better hockey than he did last night."

Born in tiny Minesing, Ontario, on February 2, 1891, Frank Foyston learned to play hockey on the family farm. "Frank was a born hockey player," said Harry, the youngest of Frank's seven brothers and sisters. "He was rugged and fast. He had a strong wrist shot and a great desire to win." Frank could play any forward position well. He was also a fine team player.

Foyston had turned pro with the Blueshirts in 1912. A year after winning the Stanley Cup in Toronto, he signed with the Seattle Metropolitans in the PCHA. After a so-so season with the Mets in 1915–16, the next year Frank broke out as a superstar.

Frank scored 36 goals in just 24 games in 1916–17. That ranked him third in the PCHA. With 12 assists, his 48 points also ranked third. Still, sportswriters from the PCHA cities voted for Frank as the league MVP.

The Mets finished the season on top of the PCHA, with 16 wins and only 8 losses. In the Stanley Cup series with the NHA,

Frank Foyston is standing second from the left in the back row of this photo of the Minesing hockey team, circa 1910.

Seattle faced the Montreal Canadiens.

Newsy Lalonde had led the Canadiens to a Stanley Cup victory in 1916. It was the first championship in team history. The Canadiens expected to beat Seattle in 1917 and win the Cup again. "We have not the slightest doubt about the outcome of the series," said team owner George

What's in a Name?

Hockey was still pretty new on the West Coast when the PCHA started. Teams used fancy names to give the sport a touch of class: Vancouver Millionaires, Victoria Aristocrats, Seattle Metropolitans, Portland Rosebuds. The Rosebuds got their name because Portland was known as The City of Roses.

Kennedy. His boast looked good early on. The Canadiens won the first game 8–4. But the Mets bounced back. They won the next two games 6–1 and 4–1. It took just three wins to clinch the series in those days, and Seattle was pumped up. "The players were filled to overflowing with confidence and pep," the *Seattle Post-Intelligencer* reported.

Game four got off to a fast start. The Mets had the first good chance, but the Canadiens were flying too. After a close call, Seattle's Jack Walker scooped up the puck. He led the Mets back to the attack. Jack bore down on the Canadiens defence, then slid a pass to Bernie Morris. Bernie squeezed through and moved in alone on Canadiens goalie Georges Vezina. His bullet shot beat Vezina and gave Seattle an early lead.

It was still 1–0 when the first period ended. The Mets came out hard to start the second. Frank blasted a drive right

The Seattle Metropolitans pose on the ice during the 1917 Stanley Cup series.

from the opening faceoff. It just missed going in. A few minutes later, Frank and Bernie sped away on a two-on-one break. Frank slipped a perfect pass right onto his teammate's stick and Bernie whipped another shot past Vezina. Two minutes later, Frank got a goal. The score was 3–0 and the Canadiens began to sag. It was 4–0 when the second period ended. The final score was 9–1.

"The Mets went through the defense like a tornado on wheels," said one Seattle

The Supreme Sacrifice

Scotty Davidson was killed in action on June 16, 1915. He was the first of three future Hall of Famers to die during World War I. George Richardson and Frank McGee were the others. At least 120 top Canadian hockey players fought in World War I. Fourteen of them died.

sportswriter. "They couldn't have played better if they cheated."

Seattle was the first American team ever to win the Stanley Cup. Frank Foyston scored seven goals in the series. Bernie Morris scored an amazing 14 times. He had six goals in the final game alone.

All in all, the 1916–17 season was a good one for the PCHA. But losing the Stanley Cup was just the beginning of big changes that were about to happen in the NHA.

4 The End of the NHA

More than a dozen NHA players had joined the army in the summer of 1916. Every team lost some of its players. Those who stayed behind had to play for less money. That was because attendance was down. Fans were starting to lose interest in hockey. The NHA hoped that adding a team of soldiers for the 1916–17 season would help.

The 228th Battalion had 12 players on its hockey team. Almost all of them had played in the NHA. Some had played in the PCHA. The team played its home games in Toronto. They shared the local arena with the Blueshirts.

The 228th Battalion looked like a strong team. In fact, many people thought they'd win the NHA championship. They did play well. They gave the Canadiens a tight battle for first place in the first half of the season. The most important thing was that they drew big crowds for their games. But there was still a war on. That was the most important thing to the army. In early February 1917, the 228th Battalion was ordered overseas. The players had to prepare right away for their ocean voyage to Europe. The team would not be allowed to finish the season.

The NHA had lost its most exciting team. How was the league going to finish the season without them? The rest of the team owners came up with a plan. They would drop the Blueshirts from the NHA too. Then they would split Toronto's players among the four remaining teams. The Quebec Bulldogs, the Montreal Canadiens, the Montreal Wanderers, and the Ottawa Senators would finish the season by themselves.

Eddie Livingstone was the owner of the Toronto Blueshirts. Obviously, he didn't like the plan. The other owners didn't even pay him to use his players. All he got was a promise that he could have his team back in time for the next season. But there never was a next season for the NHA. By the time the 1917–18 season began, the National Hockey Association was gone. It was replaced by the National Hockey *League*.

The other NHA owners had never liked Eddie Livingstone. They thought he was too hard to get along with. "He was always arguing about everything," said the

Split Decision

No leagues had playoffs in the early days of hockey. The champion was always the team that finished the season in first place. (Playoff games were held only if two teams tied for first.) In the 1916–17 season, the NHA invented a new way to have a playoff. The season was split into two halves. At the end of the season, the first-place team from the first half met the team in first place from the second half in the playoffs. Modern-style playoffs were invented by the PCHA the next year.

owner of the Ottawa Senators.

Getting rid of Livingstone was the main reason the NHL was formed. Toronto was in the new league, but Livingstone was not. The group that owned the arena the team played in bought the Blueshirts. The team soon became known as the Toronto Arenas.

Not much changed though. The NHL

faced the same player shortage as the NHA. In fact, there were fewer players available than ever. The Canadian army needed more soldiers. A new law was passed that allowed the government to draft people into the army. It was known as Conscription. Conscription practically forced men to sign up for the army. The only way around it was to prove that your job helped in the war effort. Or to take a new job that did. More hockey players decided to join the army. Others got jobs that kept them off the ice.

Conscription was going to make it harder than ever to put a full team on the ice. The Montreal Wanderers had hoped to keep the players they got from the Blueshirts. Once Toronto joined the NHL, those players had to go back. The Quebec Bulldogs had hoped to add new players from a local amateur team. They weren't able to get a single one. So the Bulldogs dropped out of the NHL. Quebec's players got divided up among the other four teams.

Two former Quebec players, Joe Malone and Jack McDonald, worked at jobs in Montreal. It made sense for them to play for the teams in that city. There was a draw to see which team would get first pick. The Canadiens won the draw and took Joe Malone.

When the rest of Quebec's players were divided up, the Canadiens also got Joe Hall. Sportswriters knew right away what that meant.

"The acquisition of Hall by the Canadiens will bring about an odd situation," the *Montreal Herald* reported. "His dozens of fights with Newsy Lalonde are a part of hockey history. Under this latest shakeup, these two will now be teammates."

Joe Hall, pictured in his Montreal Canadiens uniform in 1919.

5 The NHL Takes Over

The feud between Newsy Lalonde and Joe Hall had raged since 1914. "One night, he nearly crushed my windpipe," Newsy would later recall. "I came back and almost broke his collarbone." Perhaps that was on the night of January 12, 1916. The two players fought twice in that game. Newsy got kicked out after the second fight. A few weeks later, on February 26, Joe was at it again. He attacked a Canadiens player as the game ended. The teams rushed together from both sides of the rink. The gloves came off and everyone started fighting. Even some fans got involved. It took the police to break up the brawl.

The Canadiens had hated Joe Hall for years. Did they really want him on their team now? Newsy was still their biggest star. Would he even agree to play with Joe? And how did Joe feel? He was nearly 36 years old. He had a wife and three young children. He had a good job with a cigar company. Perhaps it was time to retire from hockey. Canadiens owner George Kennedy didn't think so. He definitely wanted to sign Joe. Newspapers followed the story with interest.

"There seems every likelihood," said the *Montreal Herald* on December 3, 1917, "that Joe Hall and Newsy Lalonde will be teammates. Hall … has just about accepted George Kennedy's terms."

Three days later, the *Montreal Star* said

that Joe had signed with the team. "Western Wild Man to be in Canadiens Uniform Soon," read the headline. The *Herald* had a similar story. "George Kennedy of Canadiens received a telegram from Joe Hall today. It says that the 'Bad Man' will leave Brandon on Saturday night. Hall will probably be out for practice on Tuesday with the Canadiens. He'll be side by side with his dear friend Newsy Lalonde."

Despite all the buildup, everything went smoothly when Newsy and Joe finally met. They got together in the dressing room before practice and shook hands. "Newsy and Hall Made Peace," wrote the *Herald*. "I'd rather have you with me than against me," they were quoted as saying. "And they both meant it," the reporter said.

Many people still wondered if these two rivals could really get along. Yet Joe and

Newsy became close friends. They even shared a room when the Canadiens travelled on road trips. Joe was still as tough as ever. Only now, when he got into trouble, Newsy was there to back him up. This led to a funny incident during a game with Toronto.

The two teams were going at each other hard, when suddenly a whistle blew. Joe knew he'd been playing rough. He figured he'd been caught doing something wrong. So he skated slowly towards the penalty box and took a seat. Newsy didn't like the call. He asked one referee what the penalty was for. The ref just shook his head. He didn't know. Newsy asked the other referee. He shook his head too. Then Newsy skated over to the penalty box. "Why'd you climb in there?" he asked. Joe was so used to getting penalties, he thought he'd been given another one! But he hadn't. The toughest player in hockey began to blush. Then he got out of the penalty box and took his spot on the ice again.

So all was well with the Montreal Canadiens. With Joe and Newsy happy, and Joe Malone in the lineup too, everyone knew they'd be a tough team to beat. The same was not true for the Montreal Wanderers. They were in trouble.

Jack of All Trades

Jack Walker had a long career in hockey. He was a big star wherever he played. He played for Seattle for nine years and helped the Mets reach the Stanley Cup Finals three times. Jack was a forward who could score goals, but he was even better at setting them up. What he was best at was shutting down the other team's top scorers. Jack is credited with inventing the hook check. He used this sweeping stick move to become one of hockey's best defensive forwards.

Two of the players they got from Quebec refused to join the team. One of their old stars had broken his leg. He was out for the entire year. Another player had a job he couldn't leave unless it was to join the army.

The Wanderers knew they needed help. They threatened to drop out of the NHL unless the other teams loaned them players. Nobody did. But when the season opened on December 19, 1917, the Wanderers were still in the league. They even beat Toronto 10–9 that night. It was the only game they ever won in the NHL.

After three straight losses, the Wanderers started complaining again. They needed more players or they would drop out. Then, on January 2, 1918, a fire broke out in the Montreal Arena. The big rink burned to the ground. Both the Canadiens and the Wanderers were left homeless. This was just the excuse the Wanderers needed.

The Canadiens moved their team to a smaller rink on the other side of Montreal, but the Wanderers dropped out of the league. The NHL would have to struggle on with only three teams: the Montreal Canadiens, the Ottawa Senators, and the Toronto Arenas.

The winter of 1917–18 was a hard one for the PCHA too. The army had taken many of its players. Two Seattle players had jobs with the Canadian National Railway. Their jobs were important enough that they didn't have to join the army ... as long as they stayed at those jobs and didn't play hockey! Jack Walker was one of those players. He was one of Seattle's top stars. Losing him was a big blow to the team and to the league.

Before the season started, the *Ottawa Journal-Press* asked, "Who would get a shock if the PCHA didn't operate this winter? Or if the Stanley Cup games had to be called off?"

There was never an army team in the PCHA. Still, the war had caused problems. The hockey arena in Victoria was taken over by the Canadian army in 1916. That meant the hockey team had to move out. The Victoria Aristocrats spent the 1916–17 season in the city of Spokane, Washington. They drew very few fans there, and decided not to stay. Since the army was still using the rink in Victoria, the Aristocrats couldn't go back there. The PCHA did play that winter, but with only three teams: Seattle, Portland, and Vancouver. There were now just six teams in all of professional hockey. A few years earlier, there had been ten. The war had cut pro hockey almost in half.

Despite the problems, the 1917–18 season was an exciting one in both leagues. After winning the Stanley Cup the year before, the Seattle Mets followed up with another first-place finish in their league. However, this was the first season for the PCHA playoffs. Seattle had to face Vancouver, and the Millionaires knocked out the Mets. The NHL still used the split-season format from the NHA. The Canadiens won the first half of the season, and Toronto won the second. Then, Eddie Livingstone's former team beat the Canadiens to win the NHL championship. Toronto capped off the strange season by beating Vancouver for the Stanley Cup.

Usually, when the hockey season ended, Frank Foyston went home to Minesing. It was a long way from Seattle, but his help was always needed on the farm. Farming was vital to the country during the war. Even so, the new law meant that Frank had to register his name with the army in the fall of 1917. He was allowed to play hockey that winter, but he didn't get to go home in the spring. The army called him up for service on April 2, 1918, just a few days after the hockey season ended. In May, Frank switched from the army to the air force. He spent the next seven months at a base in Toronto. Frank was never sent to fight in Europe before the war ended.

6 The New Danger

It wasn't easy, but pro hockey had survived another winter. By the summer of 1918, there was even reason to get excited. It finally looked like the war might soon be over. Maybe the players who had joined the army would be back when the season started in December! But December was still a long way off. And something strange was happening to the armies in Europe.

During the spring of 1918, more and more soldiers were in the hospital. They weren't suffering from war wounds. It was some kind of sickness. At first, it didn't seem too serious. Then people started to die. Some kind of horrible new flu was killing young, healthy people.

The disease spread quickly across Europe. It hit Spain hard in May. As many as eight million people in Spain were sick that month. Spanish King Alfonso XIII was among the ill. In the rest of Europe, very little was said about the disease. Their newspapers didn't want to print stories that might harm people's morale. But Spain wasn't fighting in World War I. Its newspapers printed lots of stories about the sickness. As a result, the disease became known as the Spanish Influenza.

Like most types of the flu, the Spanish Flu began with a cough and a stuffy nose. Soon after that, people felt horrible pain in their joints and muscles. There was also a high fever. As the disease attacked their

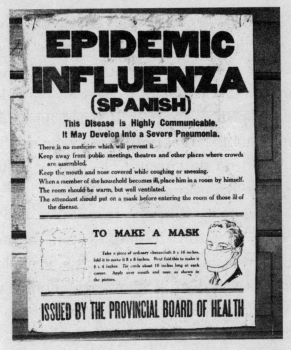

This poster warned of the dangers of the Spanish Flu and offered tips on how to prevent and treat the disease.

lungs, it became hard for patients to breathe. They might start bleeding from their nose and mouth, sometimes even from their eyes and ears. Without enough air, their skin often turned a purplish blue.

Awful as it was, most people who caught the Spanish Flu actually got better in about a week. But many people developed pneumonia. If that happened, the outlook was grim. Most of the deaths blamed on the Spanish Flu were actually caused by pneumonia.

Despite its name, the Spanish Flu didn't begin in Spain. It likely began in the United States. If not for the war, it might have stayed there. Within a few months it would have died out. Instead, the war took this flu all around the world.

The first cases of Flu were reported in February 1918. By March, several soldiers were sick at an army base called Camp Funston. When soldiers left Camp Funston for other army camps, the Flu went with them. Nobody was worried about that. Colds and flu were pretty common at army camps. With thousands of men coming together from so many places, it was expected that some germs would get passed around.

When these sick soldiers sailed to Europe in April, the Flu virus went with them. Once the virus got overseas, something terrible seemed to happen. The soldiers already fighting in Europe had been worn out by the war. Their bodies were not as strong as they should have been. The trenches they lived in were always crowded and full of disease. The battlefields they fought on were covered with rotting corpses. Maybe that was the reason the Flu became so deadly in Europe.

By the end of August, wounded soldiers coming home from the war brought the Spanish Flu back with them to North America. The first case broke out in Boston on August 31. By September, there were cases all over the eastern United

States. The same thing was true in Quebec, the Maritimes, and eastern Ontario. Slowly but surely, the disease spread west. Soon the death toll was huge.

During September and October 1918, about 8,500 people died in the city of Chicago. In New York, 851 people died in a single day! Populations weren't as big in Canadian cities, but the numbers were almost as scary. In Montreal, more than 2,800 people died. Funeral homes couldn't keep up with the numbers of bodies. In Toronto, more than 1,600 people died between October 9 and November 2. Across Canada, the Spanish Flu killed nearly 1,000 people per day in October.

The numbers of deaths were horrifying. The speed of the disease was frightening too. Some people lingered for weeks before dying, but others were dead within a few hours. A person could be healthy before breakfast, feel feverish at lunch, and die before dinner.

There were few vaccines to prevent the Flu back in 1918. There was no sure way to cure it either. And there weren't enough doctors and nurses in Canada or the United States to treat people. Medical people had been needed for the war and were still in Europe. Many of the doctors and nurses who were at home caught the Flu from their patients.

Without enough doctors and nurses, many brave people offered to help care for the sick. They sometimes ran into odd situations. "One elderly couple," recalled a volunteer worker, "was so frightened of getting germs they wouldn't let me into their house. First, I had to drink a cup of very strong coffee that was heavily laced with mustard. They thought that would kill any germs I had."

Mustard in coffee tastes horrible, but it doesn't kill germs. There was no real way to kill the flu virus. People just had to try their best not to spread it around. They were told to avoid large gatherings in public places. So, all across North America, schools, theatres, churches, department stores, and other public buildings shut down. They stayed closed for several weeks. In many cities, police were told to arrest people caught spitting in the street. When people did go outside, they were told to wear a mask over their nose and mouth. The sight of so many people in eerie white masks was hard to get used to. "It made me crazy," one woman remembered. "I was seeing ghosts in every corner of the room!"

Cases of the flu had always been dangerous. But before 1918, people who died of the flu were usually very young, or very old. Often, they were already weak or sick. With the Spanish Flu, most of the men and women who died were healthy people between the ages of 20 and 40.

Finally, in the midst of all this death and disease, the world got some wonderful news. On November 11, 1918, the guns fell silent in Europe. World War I was over.

Despite the fear of spreading germs, people in towns and cities all across North America spilled into the streets. Church bells rang out. People sang and laughed and cheered. There were parties and parades. After nearly five years, there was peace at last!

There was good news about the Spanish Flu too. It seemed to be subsiding. The *Toronto World* newspaper ran a tiny article on November 12. "Flu Outbreak Over," the headline read. "Only eight deaths were reported over the weekend. Less than 500 patients are in city hospitals. The outbreak has just about run its course."

It appeared to be true. By the beginning of December, life was pretty much back to normal. But the Spanish Flu was not done yet. It would flare up again from time to time over the next two years. When it did, the results could still be deadly. On October 13, 1918, Hamby Shore was the first pro hockey player to die of the Spanish Flu. Sadly, he would not be the last.

An Early Loss to the Flu

Hockey player Hamby Shore was 32 years old when he died of the Spanish Flu. He'd helped Ottawa win the Stanley Cup as a rookie in 1905. He had won another championship with the team in 1911. Hamby had been with the Senators when they joined the NHL. "When the whistle blows for the first game in Ottawa this winter," wrote the *Ottawa Journal* on October 15, "sports lovers won't find things quite right when Hamby Shore fails to answer the call."

7 The Peace Season

The new NHL season began on December 21, 1918. There were still only three teams in the league. But no one seemed to mind that. The war was over and the Spanish Flu seemed to be gone too. People were ready to fill their local arenas again.

The Ottawa Senators played their first home game on December 26. The *Ottawa Journal* called it "the opening of the 'peace season'." Close to 6,000 fans were in the stands. It was the biggest crowd in Ottawa in many years. Even the Duke of Devonshire, who was the Governor General at the time, was there. It was the first time since the start of World War I that he showed up to open the season. There were big cheers from the crowd when he arrived. A band played the national anthem and everybody stood. The Senators beat Toronto 5–2 that night.

A week later, on January 2, 1919, the Canadiens were in Ottawa. The crowd was even bigger that night. More than 6,000 people filled the stands. Once again, the Governor General was there. This time he dropped the puck for the ceremonial faceoff. Then Senators captain Eddie Gerard and the Canadiens' Newsy Lalonde led the crowd in giving him three cheers. Ottawa fans had plenty more to cheer about that night. The Senators beat the

Old Teams, New Teams

Toronto's Stanley Cup win in 1918 wasn't enough to save the team. The Arenas dropped out of the NHL in 1919. When Toronto returned the next season, the team had new owners and a new name. They were called the Toronto St. Pats. When the St. Pats were sold in 1927, the team got a brand new name. This time, they became the Toronto Maple Leafs.

The Senators in the NHL today are not the same team as the one from the old days. The original Senators dropped out of the NHL in 1934. When Ottawa got a new team in 1992, they took the old Senators name.

Canadiens 7–2.

The Senators looked like the team to beat as the season started. The Canadiens were struggling. That began to change just two days later when the Senators visited Montreal. The tiny Jubilee rink held only 2,500 people, but it was packed that night. Cold weather meant the ice was hard and fast.

A win by Ottawa would give them a big lead in the standings. The Canadiens couldn't let that happen, so they came out flying. They were buzzing around the Ottawa net, but they couldn't score. Then when Ottawa went on the attack, goalie Georges Vezina kept them off the score sheet too.

Vezina's Trophy

Georges Vezina joined the Canadiens in 1910. He never missed a game for the next 15 years! His streak finally ended on November 28, 1925. Chest pains forced him out of action that night. He never played another game. Vezina died of lung disease on March 26, 1926. The Vezina Trophy was donated in his memory. It has gone to the NHL's best goalie every year since the 1926–27 season.

Finally, late in the first period, Newsy scooped up the puck. He charged towards the Ottawa net, and then dropped a pass for Bert Corbeau. Corbeau fired a shot, but it was stopped. Newsy pounced on the rebound. With a flick of his wrists, he drove the puck into the net! The Canadiens were ahead 1–0.

Ottawa tied the score early in the second period, but the Canadiens were in control. They broke the game wide open in the third. The Canadiens got four goals in less than three minutes. The final score was 5–2.

The win that night started a winning streak. The Canadiens won four in a row. A fifth straight win on January 18 would clinch first place in the first-half standings. The Senators were at the Jubilee rink again. They were in for another tough night. "Right from the start of play," said the *Montreal Gazette*, "the Canadiens forced the pace."

Newsy won the opening faceoff and rushed towards the Ottawa end. He nearly set up a teammate for a goal just a few seconds later. The Canadiens kept the pressure on. When the Senators finally cleared the puck, Joe Hall scooped it up. He brought it right back into the Ottawa end.

Joe zipped past the Ottawa forwards with a few shifty moves near centre ice. Then a quick burst of speed got him through the defence. Suddenly, he was in alone on the Ottawa goal. Joe held onto the puck until the last possible moment, drawing the goalie out of his net. Then he slammed it in! Less than two minutes into the first period, Montreal was leading 1–0.

Play raced from end to end for the next few minutes. Ottawa had some chances, but Vezina stopped them all. Midway through the period, Newsy took a pass in front of the Ottawa net and whipped the puck in for a second goal. It was all Canadiens after that. Odie Cleghorn made it 3–0 just 40 seconds later. Jack McDonald scored a fourth goal before the first period ended. The Senators showed some life in the second period, but the Canadiens shut them down in the third. When the game ended it was Canadiens 5, Senators 3. The Canadiens had won the first-half title.

Jack McDonald and Odie Cleghorn were key players for the Canadiens that year. McDonald had been the player the Montreal Wanderers got from the Quebec Bulldogs when the Canadiens got Joe Malone. He joined the Canadiens when the Wanderers folded. He had been a hero in the Bulldogs' Stanley Cup victory back in 1912. His best scoring days were behind him, but he was still a valuable veteran.

Odie Cleghorn was one of two great

hockey players in his family. His older brother Sprague was a rough defencemen like Joe Hall. Odie was a great goal scorer. Odie and Sprague had played with the Wanderers for many years. Sprague signed with Ottawa for 1918–19. Odie joined the Canadiens. His scoring skill was a big help that season because Joe Malone missed a lot of games. (Malone had a job that year that would not let him travel to road games.) Malone went from 44 goals in 20 games to just 7 goals in 8 games. Odie helped pick up the slack. He played in all 18 games that year, and scored 22 goals for the Canadiens. Newsy also had 22 goals. No one else in the NHL that year scored more than 19.

Despite their scoring stars, the Canadiens slumped in the second half of the season. Ottawa came on strong. They were led by Frank Nighbor and Cy Denneny. After Newsy and Odie, Nighbor and Denneny were the NHL's best scorers. The Senators also got a boost from the return of a former player.

Harry Broadbent had once been a promising young hockey star. Fans knew him as "Punch." He may have got his nickname because of his scoring punch. He certainly had a knack around the net. He was also pretty fast with his fists! In the summer of 1915, Punch Broadbent quit hockey to join the army. For the next three years, he fought in some of the fiercest battles of World War I. Broadbent survived the war and came home to Ottawa in January of 1919. He rejoined the Senators right away.

Broadbent seemed to help his hockey team. They had finished the first half of the season with a record of only 5 wins and 5 losses. They had 7 wins and 1 loss to win the second half-season. The Canadiens had been 7 and 3 in the first half. They slipped to 3 and 5 in the second.

It was obvious who was the hotter team when the Canadiens and Senators met in the playoffs. People predicted that Ottawa would win the series and become the NHL champion. Whichever team won would go west to face the PCHA champs for the Stanley Cup.

8 Ottawa or Montreal?

Saturday night was hockey night when the NHL playoffs began on February 22, 1919. It was going to be a best-of-seven series, and game one was in Montreal. Home ice would help the Canadiens. Some bad news for Ottawa would help even more. Frank Nighbor wasn't going to be in the lineup. On the day of the game, Nighbor's sister died of blood poisoning. He left right away to be with his family.

The weather was unusually warm in

Montreal. The ice inside the Jubilee rink was soft and sticky. Bad ice often led to bad tempers, but not this night. The game was a clean one. It started off slowly, but the action soon picked up. The Canadiens scored an early goal, but the Senators struck back quickly. When the first 20 minutes were done, Ottawa led 2–1.

The Canadiens made some lineup changes after the first period. Odie Cleghorn and Joe Malone had been riding the bench. They both came on when the second period started. It was a smart move. "The two fresh men forced the pace and soon tallied twice," reported the *Montreal Gazette*. Odie got both goals. The Canadiens were leading 3–2. Newsy Lalonde got the next goal, but the Senators scored just before the period ended. Still, the Canadiens ended the period ahead 4–3.

Newsy got another goal early in the

third period. With a two-goal lead, the Canadiens took few chances. They went into a defensive shell. Joe Hall and Bert Corbeau stood strong in front of Georges Vezina. The Senators were soon running out of steam. It took until the ten-minute mark before they finally beat Vezina. It was a fluky goal on a shot from near centre.

The Senators were within one goal, but 5–4 was as close as they got. The Canadiens went up by two goals again when Joe Malone scored. He got another one just five seconds after a faceoff. Then Newsy struck again 30 seconds after that. His third goal of the night made the final score 8–4.

Game two in the series was played in Ottawa. Nighbor was still away with his family, but Senators fans hoped they could make a difference. A big crowd packed the arena. They started making noise right from the opening faceoff. The crowd loudly begged Ottawa to get an early goal.

The Senators had plenty of good chances in the first period. Vezina stopped them all. Early in the second period, Ottawa finally went ahead. The lead didn't last long, though. Joe Malone struck back with a goal just one minute later. "Watch Malone!" the Ottawa coach yelled at his players, but the Phantom slipped around them again. His next goal put Montreal ahead 2–1. The game remained close, but three goals by Odie Cleghorn in the third period led the Canadiens to a 5–3 win.

The series returned to Montreal for game three. Newsy thrilled the hometown crowd with five goals that night. The Canadiens won 6–3. They led the series three games to none. It would be all over with just one more win.

Obviously, the Senators were in trouble. The only good news for Ottawa was that Frank Nighbor was back for game four.

Short Seasons

Hockey seasons were much shorter in the early days. They could be as short as eight games. They rarely lasted longer than 20 or 24 games. Back then, cold temperatures were needed to keep the ice frozen in many cities. Seasons usually started in late December. They had to be over by the middle of March.

He was not only one of the game's best scorers, he was also hockey's best defensive centre. Nighbor kept the Canadiens bottled up.

The weather had remained mild throughout the series. In game four, tempers started to flare. There was no really rough stuff, but the referees called a lot of penalties. Art Ross was one of the referees that night. He was in his first season as a referee after many years as one of hockey's biggest stars. He and Joe Hall had been good friends for years. They had been teammates back in Brandon. Their friendship did not stop Joe from complaining about some of Art's calls that night. After one shouting match, Art got angry. He warned Joe to watch his language. When Joe kept shouting, Art gave him a five-minute penalty. Reporters asked Joe about the incident after the game. He told them he had kept his language clean. All he'd said to his old friend was this: "Why don't you grab an Ottawa uniform and a stick? You couldn't hurt us so much that way!"

The Senators scored a 6–3 win on home ice. Despite their loss in game four, the Canadiens felt sure they'd win the series. They started making reservations for the trip to the west coast. Their fans were confident too. Nearly 3,000 of them squeezed their way into the tiny Jubilee rink for game five.

Game five was played on March 6, 1919. Cold weather had returned to Montreal, and there was finally fast ice for the game. The Canadiens made good use of it. The *Montreal Gazette* wrote that the Canadiens "cut out a fast pace and were the first to attack. They smothered Ottawa with their speed." Four minutes into the first period, the Senators goalie stopped a hard shot from the side. When he tried to clear the rebound, he fell down. Newsy saw his chance. He had circled behind the net and just had to reach out front and tap the puck into the open side. Canadiens 1, Ottawa 0 — that was the score when the first period ended.

The Senators knew their season was on the line. They came out strong to start the second period. They got an early goal, and kept on pressing. Only great saves by Vezina kept the Canadiens in the game. Late in the period, Newsy set up Joe

Malone and the Canadiens were on top again. Early in the third, Bert Corbeau rushed from end to end. He put the Canadiens ahead 3–1. After another Ottawa goal, it was up to Corbeau, Hall, and Vezina to anchor the defence. They did the job until Odie Cleghorn scored to clinch it. The final score was 4–2. The Canadiens won the series four games to one.

With their quick victory, the Canadiens had a few days to rest before heading out west. They left by train on the night of March 10, 1919. A big crowd was at the station to see them off. The train was headed for Vancouver, but nobody knew yet if that was the team's final destination. The PCHA champions had yet to be crowned.

9 How the West Was Won

Frank Foyston spent the summer and fall of 1918 in the air force. He was back in Seattle for the 1918–19 season. The Mets beat the Vancouver Millionaires 4–1 in the opening game. Frank scored a goal. It was the first of 15 for him that season. It was not one of his best totals, but it still ranked him fourth in the league. Cyclone Taylor of the Millionaires was the PCHA's top scorer. He had 23 goals. He also led the league with 13 assists. Seattle and

Vancouver battled for top spot all season long. They were never more than four points apart in the standings. Usually, they were even closer than that. It was an exciting season that almost didn't happen.

If the war hadn't ended, the PCHA might have collapsed. "We were just about ready to give up," admitted PCHA president Frank Patrick. "But with players returning from the armed forces, we went to work with renewed hope."

Cyclone's Star Powers

In his day, Cyclone Taylor was the biggest star in hockey. His name made headlines everywhere he went. Taylor began his career as a defenceman. He could score goals at one end of the ice and speed back to stop them at the other. Taylor became a forward when he joined the Vancouver Millionaires. By the 1918–19 season, he'd won the PCHA scoring title five times in seven years.

Like the NHL, the PCHA had only three teams in 1918–19. Portland was gone, but Victoria was back. The army no longer needed the arena there. However, the battle with the Spanish Flu was not yet over on the west coast. It would drag on throughout the hockey season.

The first case of Spanish Flu didn't hit Seattle until October 3, 1918. That was more than a month after the Flu appeared in the east. City leaders in Seattle knew all about the horrors in eastern cities. They tried their best to keep their city safe. First, they closed the local dancehalls. Soon, schools, churches, and theatres were closed too. On October 29, 1918, it became the law for everyone in Seattle to wear a mask.

All the rules were followed at first. Things began to fall apart once the war ended. Like everywhere else, people in Seattle partied in the streets. Newspapers reported that, "there was not a mask in sight."

The next day, the mask law was lifted. Public buildings re-opened. The Flu had seemed to disappear in the east when the war ended. But the same was not true out west. Within a few days, people were getting sick. Mid-November to mid-December became a deadly time in Seattle. Life didn't start to get back to normal until January.

The Flu followed a similar path in Vancouver. The first case there was reported on October 4. Vancouver had a population of 100,000 people in 1918. About 30,000 of them caught the Spanish Flu. Nearly 1,000 people died.

In Victoria, Aristocrats captain Eddie Oatman came down with the Flu in December. He was too sick to play when the season started. He was better within a few weeks, but soon other Victoria players got sick. Lester Patrick caught the Flu right after Oatman. Lester wasn't just a player in

Victoria. He was also the team's owner, coach, and general manager. Lester took no chances when other players showed symptoms. If any player had even a hint of a fever, he was sent home to go to bed. Then the team doctor was called in.

Seven more Victoria players caught the Flu during the 1918–19 season. With prompt care, and some very good luck, not a single one of them died. But the team couldn't keep up with Seattle and Vancouver. Vancouver finished the 20-game season in first place. Their record was 12 wins and 8 losses. Seattle was close behind at 11 and 9. Victoria finished last. Their record was 7 and 13.

Playoffs in the PCHA pitted the first-place team against the second-place team. The series between the Seattle Mets and the Vancouver Millionaires began on March 12, 1919. It was just a two-game series. The total goals from both games would be added up to give one final score. As the first-place team, Vancouver got to choose which game they wanted to play at home. They picked the second game. So the series for the PCHA championship opened in Seattle.

The Seattle Arena was probably the best rink in all of North America. At this time, many arenas were still built of wood. They looked like drafty old barns. Even the arenas that were built of brick looked like factories or warehouses. The Seattle Arena was different. It had beautiful brickwork and large, arched windows. Inside, it had wide aisles that made it easy to reach the comfortable seats. There was usually room for 3,000 hockey fans. Close to 4,000 of them jammed their way inside for the playoff opener.

There wasn't much to cheer about in the first period of game one. That all changed early in the second. Frank

Foyston put Seattle on top after just 41 seconds. A few minutes later, he scored again. Frank got his third goal of the night in the third period as the Mets cruised to a 6–1 win.

The series continued two nights later in Vancouver. To win the series, the Millionaires needed to win game two by at least six goals. It wouldn't be easy, but they wouldn't go down without a fight. A quick start was important. The Millionaires began fast as lightning. The fans had barely settled into their seats when they were leaping out of them to cheer. Cyclone Taylor won the opening faceoff, and set up a goal just 12 seconds later.

The Millionaires kept up their fast pace. "Vancouver was peppering bullet shots at the Mets net," the newspapers said. A few minutes later, they scored again.

The Mets had been playing defensive hockey. They were trying to protect their big lead. It wasn't working. So they decided to change tactics. Seattle went on the attack to start the second period. They had some good chances, but they couldn't score. When Vancouver did, the score was 3–0. The score in the series was 6–4. Then Taylor scored another goal for Vancouver near the end of the second period. There was just a one-goal difference now. Seattle's big lead was nearly gone.

The Mets switched back to a defensive style for the third period. This time, it worked. The Mets scored a goal of their own. They lost the game 4–1, but they won the series 7–5.

Seattle would get to play the Canadiens for the Stanley Cup. Still, the best news in the city that month had nothing to do with hockey. It was that the Spanish Flu finally seemed to be gone. There was not a single flu-related death in Seattle during the month of March.

10 East Meets West

The Canadiens reached Vancouver on March 16. It took an entire week to travel across the country by train. For that reason, Stanley Cup games at this time were always played in just one city. The eastern champs hosted the series one year. The western champs got it the next. As the Mets were the newly crowned champions of the PCHA, Seattle was the site for the 1919 series.

After a short stay in Vancouver, the

Training on the Train

The Canadiens had to stay in shape on their way out west. So they played exhibition games. A game in Regina was between teams made up of both Canadiens players and players from Saskatchewan. In Calgary, the Canadiens beat a team of local all-stars. The score was 12–1. Their final tune-up came in Vancouver. They beat the Millionaires 4–3.

Canadiens left for Seattle on an overnight ferry. They arrived on the morning of March 18. The Stanley Cup series began the next day. Local newspapers were filled with stories about it.

Back in 1917, the Mets had beaten the Canadiens easily. But George Kennedy said things would be different this time. He told reporters that his team was at least 50 percent better than it was in 1917. "We are anxious to avenge our defeat," he said.

Kennedy predicted that the Canadiens would take the Stanley Cup with them back to Montreal.

Mets coach Pete Muldoon wasn't worried. His Seattle team was considered the fastest in hockey. "We will skate the visitors off their feet," he boasted. Speed had made the difference in 1917. The Canadiens knew that. Some of their players were pretty fast too, but they had to slow down Seattle's speedy skaters. Sportswriters were pretty sure how they'd try to do it.

"Newsy Lalonde and Bad Joe Hall are known to be rough customers," reported the *Seattle Post-Intelligencer*. "Should they feel inclined to lay the wood too heavily, the Seattle squad will be in a sorry way." The *Seattle Times* was worried too. "Lalonde and Hall have a record of being the bad men of eastern hockey. It's not unlikely they will get in some rough work here too." Bert Corbeau was also a player to watch out for. "He'll be the heaviest man on the ice," the *Times* told its readers. "He tips the scales at 185 pounds and uses his weight to good advantage. He is just as dangerous as Bad Joe Hall."

But the first game of the Stanley Cup series wasn't rough at all. In fact, not a single penalty was called. Both teams simply relied on their speed. The result was a disaster for the Canadiens. The Mets won the game 7–0. Frank Foyston and Jack Walker were the big stars for Seattle. Frank scored three goals for the Mets. Jack had only one, but his tricky hook check kept the Canadiens bottled up.

Despite the score, even the Seattle newspapers said the game was closer than it seemed. It was goaltending that made the difference. Georges Vezina had a terrible night. Seattle's Harry Holmes played the game of his life.

"We were beaten," George Kennedy told the reporters, "but not by any 7 to 0 margin. If Holmes had not played such a sensational game, we would have scored at least six goals." Kennedy vowed that his team would do better in game two. "The boys are not discouraged," he said. "They'll go into the next game with lots of confidence. I look for them to win it."

The Canadiens would have one big advantage in the second game. It was going to be played with NHL rules. PCHA rules had been used in game one. The rules of the two leagues had a few key differences. For one thing, the PCHA still used a rover. Someone playing this position lined up between the defence and the forwards. He could drop back to help the defence or head up ice to join the attack. The NHA stopped using the rover in 1911–12. The PCHA used the rover right through the 1921–22 season. That meant there had been seven players on the ice instead of six per team.

Even more important, the rules about passing the puck were different. In the early days of hockey, forward passing was not allowed. The only way to advance the puck was by skating with it. The PCHA was the first league to allow forward passing, but it was allowed only in the centre zone between the two blue lines. The 1918–19 season was the first time the NHL allowed forward passing. However, the zone between the blue lines was only 40 feet (12 m) wide in the NHL. It was 60 feet (18 m) wide in the PCHA. A speedy team like Seattle could use that extra room to zoom up the ice even quicker. In game two, the Mets would have to adjust their style to the smaller NHL zone.

The change in rules made a difference.

Built in 1915, the Seattle Arena was a much fancier-looking building than most other hockey arenas of its day.

The Canadiens played a much better game. They beat the Mets 4–2 and tied up the series. "It was the Canadiens' game from the very first period," admitted the *Seattle Times.* "Better yet, it was Newsy Lalonde's game." Newsy scored all four Canadiens goals. "Lalonde played rough, aggressive hockey," the *Post* reported. "The dark-haired leader of the visitors was impossible to stop when he gained the puck."

Only one penalty was called in game two, but the newspapers said the play was rough. Game three was the roughest yet.

"Last night's struggle was a hard-checking affair," the *Post* said after game three. "The play was rough and spills were frequent."

"Sticks flew in every direction," said the *Times*. "Heavy body checks and slashing kept the penalty box filled." Joe Hall certainly lived up to his reputation as a hard hitter. Joe played a rough game, but kept it clean. "He was in every mix-up," said the *Times*, "but was only sent to the penalty box once."

All the rough stuff in game three didn't seem to slow down Seattle. Playing by the PCHA rules again, the Mets won 7–2. It was another bad night for Vezina. Frank

Foyston beat him four times. He also got an assist. "Foyston's work was especially brilliant," said the reporter from the *Times*.

Seattle was now just one win away from the Stanley Cup.

11 Working Overtime

By the end of game three of the Stanley Cup playoffs, the rough play was taking its toll. Joe Hall was getting battered and bruised. So was Seattle tough guy Cully Wilson. They were both expected to play in game four, but not other players. Bert Corbeau had a badly sprained shoulder. No one was sure if he could play. The same was true for Seattle's top two defencemen. Roy Rickey and Bobby Rowe both had injured ankles. It was good for both teams that game four was played with NHL rules. They had to put only six players on the ice.

When game four began on March 26, Bobby Rowe was in uniform. But the Mets hoped they wouldn't have to use him. The other wounded players were all in the starting lineup. The game they played in was something special. "They may play hockey for the next 1,000 years," wrote a sportswriter in the *Seattle Post-Intelligencer*, "but they'll never stage a greater struggle than last night's."

Play began with Frank and Newsy taking the opening faceoff. Frank got to the puck first, and pulled it behind him. Cully Wilson scooped it up and raced towards the Canadiens end. He fired a shot, but Vezina handled it. Then Newsy led a rush on the Mets net, but Holmes blocked his shot with no trouble. Odie Cleghorn had a good chance, but Holmes stopped him too. He was having another good game. This time, Vezina matched him save for save.

The play raced from end to end, but there were plenty of hard hits too. "Players were being sent spinning," said the *Times*. At one point, Joe Hall hit Frank Foyston so hard that both players seemed dizzy for a minute.

As time was running out in the first period, Odie sped in on the Seattle net. It looked like he had a sure goal, but Holmes made another great save. Then Muzz Murray picked up the puck. He was playing defence in place of Bobby Rowe. Murray carried the puck up the ice. When he got into the Canadiens end, he whipped a pass to Cully Wilson. Wilson beat Vezina with a quick shot and the Seattle fans jumped to their feet. But Wilson's shot wasn't quite quick enough. The first period ended a half-second before the puck went in. Wilson's goal didn't count. There was no score.

Play remained even in the second period. Both teams had more good chances, but neither one scored. The third period was scoreless too. So the game went into overtime.

The Canadiens needed a goal to stay alive. If the Mets scored, they would be the Stanley Cup champions. But the Seattle players were worn out. Without Bobby Rowe, they'd played the game with just one substitute player. But Foyston had hurt his leg in the third period, so now there was no one left on the bench. When Cully Wilson got hurt in overtime, Rowe had to limp out onto the ice.

Amazingly, the Mets managed to hang on. The Canadiens were pretty tired too. According to the *Post*, "Both teams struggled until their tongues hung out." Yet they still sped from end to end. "The fans cheered wildly when a Mets skater dashed down the ice. They held their breath nervously when someone charged the Seattle net."

The teams played ten minutes of overtime, and no one scored. So they played ten minutes more. When there was still no goal, the game was declared a 0–0 tie.

How could a playoff game end in a tie? It was because of a mistake by PCHA officials. They believed it was the NHL rule to play no more than 20 minutes of overtime. That wasn't true. Just like an NHL playoff game today, the match should have continued until somebody scored … no matter how long it took.

"It was the hardest-played game in hockey history," said PCHA president Frank Patrick. Yet the game had decided nothing. The battle would start all over again when the two teams met in game five.

Both teams were glad to have two days off before they had to play again. Neither team spent very much of that time on the ice. Players on both sides needed to rest more than they needed to practice.

On the Seattle side, Frank had suffered an injury to his thigh. The team doctor was working hard to get him ready for game five. Bobby Rowe's bruised ankle was still bothering him. Roy Rickey's was sore too, yet he had stayed on the ice for all 80 minutes of game four. No one else on either team had done that. Jack Walker was cut above the eye during game four, but he was all right.

The Canadiens still had Corbeau to worry about. He hadn't played much in game four, but his shoulder wasn't getting better. Other players had some cuts and bruises, but they would be fine to play.

Game five was played on Saturday

night, March 29, 1919. As in game four, a win for Seattle would mean the Stanley Cup. The Canadiens needed to win the game just to keep their hopes alive. It sure didn't look like they would do it.

Foyston put the Mets ahead 1–0 early in the first period. Then Jack Walker scored near the end of the first. Jack scored again barely a minute into the second period. It was 3–0 for Seattle when the second period ended. The Mets were only 20 minutes away from the Stanley Cup.

The Canadiens knew they were running out of time. They went on the attack as soon the third period started. Just a few minutes in, Odie Cleghorn got the puck all alone in front of the net. When he whipped a shot past Holmes, the Canadiens were finally on the scoreboard.

One minute later, the Canadiens attacked again. This time, it was Newsy who found himself alone in front of the net. He pulled goalie Holmes out of position with a nifty deke. Then he tucked the puck into the open net.

The Seattle lead was just 3–2, and the Canadiens really poured it on. The Mets didn't want to take any chances. They tried their best just to hang on. Then, with time running out, there was a scramble in front of the Mets net.

Holmes made a nice save ...

The puck rebounded into the air ...

Newsy reached up as high as he could ...

He knocked down the puck with his gloved hand ...

Then he fired a quick shot over Holmes' shoulder and into the net!

The game was tied 3–3. There were three minutes left. "The period ended with both teams fighting tooth and nail," reported the *Seattle Post-Intelligencer*. No one could score. So once again the game went into overtime.

Tired as they were after so much hockey, the two teams kept up their fast pace. "Canadiens and Mets alike tore down the ice in sensational sallies. When they lost the puck, they skated back exhausted to their defense positions," wrote the *Seattle Times*. Frank had a chance to end the game early, but Vezina stopped him. Newsy had a few good chances too, but Holmes always made the save.

After nearly 15 minutes of overtime, Frank collided with a Canadiens player near centre ice. His injured thigh took a painful pounding. Wounded and winded, Frank barely made it to the bench. Then he collapsed. Just a few seconds later, the blade snapped on Jack Walker's skate. He had to head for the bench as well. Cully Wilson had the puck in the Canadiens end and was buzzing all around the net. Then he headed for the bench too. Gasping for breath, Wilson called for help. But with Foyston hurt and Walker's skate broken, there was no one to replace him.

Jack McDonald had just stepped onto the ice for the Canadiens. He was well-rested and ready to go. When he saw the confusion at the Mets bench, he pounced on the puck. Then he headed straight for Rickey and Rowe, the Seattle defence. Despite his bad ankle, Rowe had been on the bench for just three minutes all game. Rickey hadn't been off the ice at all. After playing 80 minutes in game four, he'd played nearly 76 minutes more in game five.

McDonald sped toward the tired defencemen. He made a few shifty moves and zipped right between them. Then he went in alone on Holmes. McDonald fired a shot for the far corner … and scored!

The Canadiens' comeback was complete. They had won the game 4–3.

60-Minute Men

Teams used nine or ten players in the early days of hockey. Starters were expected to play the full 60 minutes. Subs got on the ice only if there was a major injury. By the 1910s, it was more common to take players off for a short rest. Still, some top stars played the full 60 minutes right into the 1920s.

Dejected, the Mets trudged back to their dressing room. Foyston's leg was so sore he almost couldn't walk. Rowe wasn't a whole lot better. Walker and Rickey weren't too bad, but they each had cuts and a lot of bruises. Wilson was pale and running a fever.

The mood was much better in the winning dressing room. Still, things weren't quite right with the Canadiens. In all the excitement, people hadn't noticed something. Joe Hall had gone off the ice midway through the second period and never come back. He was running a fever too. Like Cully Wilson, people thought Joe was just exhausted.

With two days off before the last game, everyone thought that things would be fine. Nobody seemed too worried ... but they soon would be.

12 Cancelled Cup

The final game in the Stanley Cup playoff series of 1919 was set for Tuesday, April 1. On Monday morning, Seattle newspapers were still filled with stories of Saturday's struggle. They were looking forward to Tuesday's finale.

"The Metropolitans and Les Canadiens are enjoying their much needed rest," said the reporter from the *Post*. "The Seattle players are badly banged up … Every man has lost weight in his effort to bring another championship to Seattle. Harry Holmes has lost 12 pounds. His goalie equipment weighs so much that sweat pours off his body. Roy Rickey is 10 pounds lighter than when the series started. Frank Foyston and Jack Walker's faces are pale. They both show the result of hard playing."

The *Times* was more worried about injuries than weight loss. "Foyston, with his leg badly wrenched, is the worst injured of the Mets. Bobby Rowe and his bad ankle come next on the list."

The *Times* said very little about the Canadiens. The *Post* confirmed that Joe Hall did have a high fever, but no one doubted that the game would go on. "Both teams are a weary looking bunch, but neither squad lacks the determination to win the final game. Both teams say that their players are out to win tomorrow at all costs."

The mood had changed by the end of the day. The reporters sending stories back to Montreal were a lot more worried about Joe Hall's condition. "He is seriously ill," they said, "and unable to leave his bed." Jack McDonald had a high fever too.

That night, things took a turn for the worse. George Kennedy, Newsy Lalonde, and two other Canadiens players developed fevers. It wasn't just because they were tired. It was something much worse. The Canadiens had the Spanish Flu.

By the morning of April 1, the team was in no condition to play hockey. There were five sick players on the nine-man roster. George Kennedy still hoped to save the final game. He wanted to borrow players from Victoria to replace his sick men. Pete Muldoon, the Seattle coach, didn't like that plan. He thought it would give his own team an unfair advantage. He felt it wouldn't be right to win like that.

PCHA president Frank Patrick was the man in charge of the Stanley Cup series. He was the one who had to decide. Patrick felt the best thing to do would be to delay the game for 24 hours. Then, after a doctor examined the players, he would make a final decision. However, by 2:30 that afternoon, it was obvious what the decision had to be. The players were much too sick to play. The arena would be a breeding ground for dangerous germs. The final game had to be called off.

Since it was the Canadiens who couldn't play, some people thought Seattle should win the series by default. Patrick said the PCHA did not want to claim a victory that way.

There would be no winning team decided for 1919. For the first time in hockey history, the Stanley Cup was cancelled.

Though the series was over, the eyes of

hockey fans were still on Seattle. Only now, instead of waiting to get the score, people were waiting for medical reports. Telegrams and telephone calls whirred across the wires between Seattle and Montreal. Newspapers all across Canada did their best to keep readers up to date. It wasn't easy because the news changed fast.

On the night of April 1, when they should have been playing the final game, Joe Hall and Jack McDonald were taken to the hospital. Their fevers were at nearly 105° F (40° C). The other Canadiens who were sick stayed in their beds at the Georgian Hotel.

By the morning of April 2, Odie Cleghorn was sick too. Then, on April 3, Pete Muldoon came down with the Spanish Flu. So did Roy Rickey and Muzz Murray. Frank Foyston didn't have the Flu, but his thigh injury had become much worse. Doctors had to wrap his leg in

STANLEY CUP SERIES IS OFF

Five Canadiens and Manager
Are Very Ill With
Influenza

EACH TEAM WINS TWICE

Lalonde, Hall, Couture, Ber-
linquette and McDonald
Have Temperature
of 101-5

*News that the Stanley Cup series was cancelled made
headlines in papers all across Canada. This one
appeared in Toronto's* Globe *newspaper on April 2,
1919.*

bandages to prevent more trouble.

The worst news was about Joe Hall and
Jack McDonald. They were both
"dangerously ill." Doctors were very
worried about Joe. His disease had
developed into pneumonia. A message was
sent to Joe's family. If they wanted to see

Victims of Victoria?

There have been stories that the Canadiens caught the Spanish Flu in Victoria. People thought so because so many Victoria players had been sick. But the Canadiens went to Seattle straight from Vancouver. Their ship never even stopped in Victoria!

him, they'd better come quickly.

Some of Joe's relatives lived in Vancouver. His wife's parents did too. Joe's mother and his brother left Vancouver right away. They made it to Seattle in a couple of hours. Joe's wife and his three children had to come all the way from Brandon. It would be two or three days before they could get there.

By April 4, almost everyone was getting better. Even Jack McDonald was starting to improve. Only Joe Hall's condition was worse. His temperature had dropped a little, but it was still a dangerous 103° F (39° C). There was fluid in his lungs. It was getting harder and harder for him to breathe. There was little his doctor could do for him.

Everyone knew that Bad Joe Hall was as tough as they come. Yet this was a fight he couldn't win. He died at 2:30 p.m. on Saturday, April 5, 1919.

"Joe Hall was one of the real veterans of hockey," Frank Patrick said. "The game has suffered a loss by his passing."

Epilogue

Joe Hall was not quite 37 years old when he died. His mother was at his side. His wife and children didn't make it in time. They were still on the train when they got the bad news in a telegram. They arrived in Vancouver the next morning. Joe's mother and brother brought his body there. The family held his funeral in Vancouver on April 8, 1919. Joe's wife would stay in Vancouver with her children. She raised their family there.

Newsy Lalonde was at Joe's funeral. He'd been back on his feet for just a couple of days. Still, he wanted to pay his respects to a bitter rival who'd become a good friend. Newsy was one of the six men who helped carry Joe's coffin to the grave.

Newsy got over his case of the Spanish Flu quickly. The other players all got better too. George Kennedy wasn't as lucky. Though he seemed to be fine at first, he never fully recovered. Kennedy died on October 19, 1921. He was only 39.

Newsy remained with the Canadiens through the 1921–22 season. His final NHL season came in 1926–27. In all, he played 99 games in the NHL. He scored 124 goals. Newsy scored more than 400 goals during his pro hockey career. Joe Malone was the only other player from that era who even scored 300. Both of them were elected to the Hockey Hall of

Fame in 1950.

Newsy remained a Canadiens fan his whole life. As an old man, he was often in the crowd in Montreal. Newsy died on November 20, 1971. He was 84 years old.

Like Newsy Lalonde, Frank Foyston played well into the 1920s. He showed no ill effects from his 1919 leg injury. The next year, he scored 26 goals in 22 games. That tied him for the PCHA lead. He scored 26 again in 1920–21 and led the league all by himself. Frank and Jack Walker both starred in Seattle until the team went out of business in 1924.

The PCHA broke up when Seattle folded. Vancouver and Victoria joined four other teams in the Western Canada Hockey League. Frank, Jack, and Harry Holmes all signed with Victoria. They helped their new team win the Stanley Cup in 1925. It was the last time a non-NHL team ever won the Stanley Cup.

When his playing days were done, Frank lived the rest of his life just outside Seattle. He coached hockey for a few years in the 1930s. Mostly he worked on the farm he bought there. Frank was elected to the Hockey Hall of Fame in 1958. He died on January 19, 1966, at the age of 74.

Though Joe Hall died in 1919, old-time hockey players never forgot him. Cyclone Taylor had been his teammate back in 1906. He always believed that Bad Joe Hall wasn't nearly as bad as people said. Taylor helped get Joe elected to the Hockey Hall of Fame in 1961.

Joe Malone was another player who believed that Bad Joe was a bad rap. Between the Bulldogs and the Canadiens, the two Joes were teammates for nine years. Shortly before he died in 1969, Malone talked about his old friend with hockey writer Stan Fischler. "Joe wasn't mean," Malone told him. "He liked to deal out a heavy check, but he was always ready to take it as well."

Malone told Fischler that he was very sad when Joe died. It wasn't just because he lost a friend. It was because he believed that Joe never got the chance to outlive his bad reputation. "There were plenty of rough characters on the ice in Joe's time. He was able to stay in there with all of them for more than 18 years. His death was a tragic and shocking end to the 1919 Stanley Cup series."

World War I and the Spanish Flu marked one of the worst times in hockey history. They were terrible times for people everywhere. Life was hard in those days, and often unforgiving. Just being tough wasn't always enough.

By the start of the 1920s, the whole world seemed ready for a party. The new decade became known as the Roaring Twenties. Everything seemed to get bigger and better. Cars were faster. Music was jazzier. Movies began to talk. No one wanted to remember the war or the Flu. They just wanted to have fun. Sports became bigger and better too. Babe Ruth hit baseballs further than anyone had ever seen. Football, boxing, golf, and tennis all had their own superstars. There were new superstars in hockey as well. Speedsters like Howie Morenz replaced old-timers like Newsy Lalonde. Tough guys like Eddie Shore made sure the game never lacked muscle.

The NHL began to expand in the 1920s. New teams were added in the United States — the Boston Bruins, the New York Rangers. Soon there were teams in Detroit and Chicago too. By 1926, the NHL had grown to ten teams. The leagues out west couldn't keep up. The NHL became pro hockey's only major league.

But the good times didn't last. The Roaring Twenties gave way to the Dirty Thirties. The stock market crashed and droughts ruined crops. Farms were destroyed. Companies went bankrupt. People lost their jobs. Once again, hockey was hit hard. Some teams had to fold. Soon, there were just six teams left in the NHL.

From 1939 to 1945, the world was at war for a second time. Just as before, many hockey players quit the game to join the army during World War II. Through it all, fans kept cheering for their favourite teams. The importance of the Stanley Cup continued to grow. The NHL kept growing too.

The modern NHL would shock the men who fought for the Cup in 1919. The speed of the game would dazzle them. The big crowds at the rink would amaze them. The huge salaries would stun them. The fact that a lockout could cancel the Cup would disappoint them. Only a true matter of life and death had cancelled the Cup in their day.

Today, as 30 NHL teams battle for it every year, the Stanley Cup is one of the most important trophies in all of sports. Its long history and storied past have helped make it that way.

Glossary

Amateur: A person who is not paid money to do something, such as playing a sport.

Assist: A pass that leads to a teammate scoring a goal.

Conscription: A law that forces citizens to serve in the armed forces during times of war.

Deke: To quickly pretend to move in one direction in order to trick an opponent into going the wrong way.

Defencemen: A player who plays defence

Era: A certain period of time.

Exhibition Game: A game that is not part of the regular season or playoffs.

Faceoff: To drop the puck between two opposing centres, either to start a game or to restart the action after play has been stopped.

Morale: The level of confidence or optimism felt by a person or a group of people.

MVP: Most Valuable Player.

Points: For players, the number of points awarded is the total number of goals and assists they get. For teams, two points are awarded for each game they win.

Professional: A person who is paid money to do a job or play a sport.

Rookie: Somebody who is new to an activity or job. In sports, a rookie is a person who is in his or her first year of professional play

Telegraph: A way to send telegram messages long distances through special wires.

Veteran: Somebody who has a lot of experience in an activity, or has played a sport for a long time.

Volunteer: To do something by choice, without being forced.

Acknowledgements

It was about 1973 when I first learned that the 1919 Stanley Cup Final had been cancelled. My parents had bought my brothers and me a set of miniature NHL trophies. I still have our mini Stanley Cup. What's engraved on it for the 1918–19 season are the words *No Decision*. My ten-year-old self would have loved reading this book to find out why.

A lot of people helped with this. Fellow members of the Society for International Hockey Research (SIHR) Ernie Fitz-simmons, Paul Kitchen, Bill Sproule, and Jason Wilson were always quick to answer my questions. The sad fact is, much of what they helped me with didn't make it into the final version, but I wouldn't have been able to get it done without them. Borden Mills, another SIHR member, was the one who first suggested I write about Bad Joe Hall. I have also enjoyed swapping stories about Seattle hockey with Jeff Obermeyer. He was a great help on this project. Thank you all.

Craig Campbell at the Hockey Hall of Fame gets a big assist too. I have always appreciated the access to the archives that he and Phil Pritchard have allowed me. In this case, Craig also introduced me to Larry Hall, grandson of Joe Hall. Many of the quotes by and about Joe Hall in this book come from the Joe Hall scrapbook Craig and Larry shared with me. Many of the quotes attributed to Newsy Lalonde come from Stan Fischler's book, *Heroes and History: Voices From the NHL's Past*. Thank you also to Chris MacBain at the Simcoe County Archives, where I found wonderful information about Frank Foyston.

Finally, thank you to Faye Smailes. At times, getting through this one involved being my coach as much as being my editor.

About the Author

ERIC ZWEIG is a managing editor with Dan Diamond and Associates, consulting publishers to the NHL. He has written about sports and sports history for many major publications, including the Toronto Star and The Globe and Mail. He has also been a writer/producer with CBC Radio Sports and TSN SportsRadio, and has written several popular books about hockey for both adults and children. He lives in Owen Sound, Ontario, with his family.

Photo Credits

We gratefully acknowledge the following sources for permission to reproduce the images within this book.

Glenbow Museum: p 59
The Globe and Mail: p 119
Hockey Hall of Fame: p 37, p 46, front cover top
James Foyston: p 33
Jeff Obermeyer, Seattlehockey.net: p 99
Library and Archives Canada: p 11
Montreal Herald: p 27
Simcoe County Archives: p 35
Eric Zweig: p 18, p 22

Index